A New University

A New University

The Inauguration of

Rhoten A. Smith as Sixth President of Northern Illinois University

Northern Illinois University Press, DeKalb, Illinois

Contents

Introduction

A New University

Arra M. Garab

Associate Professor of English

As its title indicates, this book is focused on an inspiring phenomenon of our time: the emergence of a new university especially relevant to the needs of our changing culture and responsive to the growing requirements of an increasingly aware citizenry. *A New University* celebrates the coming to age of an ambitious institution. And it marks as well the faithful commitment of Northern Illinois University to the inherited trust of a deeply-rooted American tradition.

From its beginnings, our nation has placed great emphasis on higher education. Sending its young college graduates westward to found new colleges and academies, often even before the land was cleared and properly settled, the young republic knew well the importance of an educated electorate. Thomas Jefferson, for example, chose to be remembered as the founder of the University of Virginia rather than for a host of more celebrated and unique accomplishments. Embodying at once the resplendent attainments of the Renaissance as well as of the Enlightenment of his own time, in which he figured so prominently, he urged the nurturing of a "natural aristocracy of intellect," and insisted that its broad membership be drawn from the popular base upon which democratic society must rest.

From the days of the infant republic, we as a nation have rested much of our hope and invested much of our energy in the furthering of enlightened ideals such as those of Jefferson. "Excellence and Opportunity," the theme of the inauguration of Northern Illinois University's sixth president and of this commemorative book as well, presents a paradox analogous to Jefferson's "natural aristocracy of intellect." Compounded of seemingly antithetical elements, "Excellence and Opportunity" is precisely the sort of paradox that has stirred the imagination and quickened the creative zeal of thinkers and artists across the centuries. Summations of subtle complexities and symbols of their generative power, certain paradoxes can become means of insight and progress. Just as men have held that the meek shall inherit the earth, and, like Jefferson, have upheld exclusiveness provided that it not disdain inclusiveness, so too we as a university hold that an excellent university is a magnanimous one, that its bigness of soul may be measured largely by the magnitude of its social responsibility.

The successive and successful metamorphoses of Northern Illinois University reflect the enthusiastic response of an enlightened state to the developing needs of a promising region. Founded in 1895 as Northern Illinois State Normal School, in 1921 it became Northern Illinois State Teachers College and recorded an enrollment of 402. In 1955 it changed its name to Northern Illinois State College, and two years later it became Northern Illinois University. In 1962 four departments were approved for doctoral programs by the North Central Association. The institution was for many years under the aegis of the Board of Governors of State Colleges and Universities. In 1967, when enrollment reached 18,057, it was placed under the governance of the newly-created Board of Regents, whose chairman, Dr. Norris L Brookens, a noted specialist in internal medicine at the Carle Clinic in Urbana as well as an experienced educator, invested Rhoten A. Smith as sixth president of the university on May 24, 1968.

Born in Dallas, Texas, in 1921, President Smith received his B.A. and M.A. from the University of Kansas; and in 1954, upon completing his dissertation on majority rule in American democratic theory, he was awarded his Ph.D. by the University of California. He taught at the University of Kansas until 1958, when he was appointed by New York University as Professor of Politics in the Law School and the Graduate School of Arts and Sciences. From 1961 to 1967 he was Dean of the College of Liberal Arts of Temple University, attracting much attention and winning wide acclaim not only for the excellent rapport he achieved with his faculty colleagues and administrative

associates, but also for his role in furthering the remarkable growth of that university.

Selected after a nationwide search conducted by an elected faculty committee, President Smith assumed the duties of his office in September, 1967, and quickly won considerable support from all segments of the academic community, as well as from townspeople who have responded heartily to his grasp of common problems. He was warmly welcomed by the student body, who quickly became aware of the new style he brought to the campus. And the faculty and administration, responsive to the imaginative goals and vigorous thrust of his leadership, have joined him in engaging the many complex problems that Northern Illinois University must discover, face, and master as it enters the most challenging and rewarding years of its full maturity.

This book represents an effort to preserve not only the spirit of President Smith's inauguration, but something of its substance as well. For nearly a week the university community and their guests participated in a variety of events; the material selected for presentation here suggests but a part of the multifold activity of that week. Victor G. Rosenblum's statement is taken from the introduction to his Phi Beta Kappa lecture, "Redress for the Alienated: Law and the Revolution." Professor of Political Science at Northwestern University at the time of his lecture, he is now president of Reed College. The inauguration lecture was delivered by Percy L. Julian, director of the Julian Research Institute and president of Julian Associates. His distinguished career as a research chemist and consultant has been recognized by a dozen honorary degrees and by membership on the Board of Regents. Samuel H. Shapiro, Governor of Illinois, and Willard Wirtz, Secretary of Labor and a former Northern Illinois University student, brought greetings from their respective governmental bodies.

President Smith's inaugural address, "Excellence and Opportunity," hopefully inaugurates a new era in the already eventful history of Northern Illinois University. At a time when the national need for greater excellence and increased opportunity in higher education is more pressing than ever, he takes on the challenge of leading this university through perhaps the most crucial stage of its development. As he has frequently stressed, at various times in its history Northern Illinois University has been called upon to perform various missions, and has done so exceedingly well. Now, with nearly twenty thousand students and a faculty of well over a thousand, it has accepted a new mission and a mandate to fulfill that mission imaginatively, effectively, and enthusiastically.

We join him now in "laying our hands" to the dedicated task of shaping a new university. With him we believe that excellence of academic witness entails unusual sensitivity to the temper of our time, that responsible academic governance involves unusual concern for the expansion of opportunity, and that a new university relevant to a new time will muster much faith in its pursuit of both excellence and opportunity ❧

Inaugural Events

Redress for the Alienated

Victor G. Rosenblum

President of Reed College

Many sectors of our world are permeated by moods of hostility and polarization as hallmarks of our time. It was especially depressing to see the President of the United States conveying, and until very recently escalating, anger and frustration rather than spurs to reform; and this mood has been imposed on some universities as well, as institutions dedicated to intellectual confrontations have been sapped of their intellectuality and have succumbed to the picaresque and Pinteresque in the world about us. We need no new demonstrations of the capacity of human beings to be inhuman. Yet man could not have been made to deny his humanity; he could not have been

16

conceived for the purpose of being overwhelmed by his ecology. This is one reason why I am proud to have been a Northwestern faculty member; for as a result of trends begun several years ago (and initiated in some measure by NIU's Dean Richard Bowers, then on the Northwestern staff) the officials of the university were geared to respond to crisis with restraint, compassion, and a sense of trusteeship rather than with immediate insistence upon enforcement of property rights. Among other things, the university recognized that students should have the right to live where they want to live, even though we might believe that a desire on the part of black students for racially segregated living is misguided. Law and order are of course essential to democratic society, but the message of law and order must be conveyed not merely to the oppressed and alienated but to the power structure as well. The realtor who violates a fair-housing ordinance, the school board that ignores a judicial order to integrate, the policeman who uses more force than is necessary need to hear the message of law and order at least as much as those whose aspirations for equality were so long deflected and suppressed.

Enlarging upon views I expressed in the annual Law Day issue of the *Chicago Daily Law Bulletin* last month, I want to deal tonight with some developments in law as an instrument of redress and alternative to revolution. Genuine equality before the law must be a hallmark of the just society, and equality of access to the judicial and administrative mechanisms of the law is a *sine qua non* for oper-

ationalizing the equity principle. This is not to say that the legislature and the executive are unimportant insofar as extinguishing the debilitating effects of poverty is concerned; it is to say, rather, that the development of a participative assertiveness by the poor in the ongoing processes of policy making and conflict resolution cannot be achieved without equality of access to those mechanisms of policy formation and execution that have direct impact on individual lives. We're all aware of the perversions which laws have been used to support in the past—from Runaway Slave Acts to the infamous Nuremberg Laws. Even reforms were often illusory.

Legal aid movements in the past were often characterized by an unctuous good will, serving more to gratify lawyers' needs for benchmarks to record their own mobility and affluence than as instruments of innovation and reform. The lawyer who volunteered for legal aid work experienced a maximum of moral self-righteousness and a minimum of personal inconvenience. Legal aid offices were centered exclusively in central business districts, enabling the volunteer lawyer to commute quickly from his commercial law office and ensuring the insulation of the legal aid office from all but the most mobile of the poverty-stricken. There were no devices for giving visibility to problems of those within the inner ghettoes. Despite noble efforts by many outstanding and dedicated men in the legal aid field, the output of legal aid as a component of the legal system had to be measured in terms of numbers of cases handled rather than by degree of impact on the lives of clients or changes in legal norms.

I would not contend that all of this has changed today, but recent trends and patterns indicate that change is both feasible and imminent. The growth of neighborhood legal services—from pioneering projects several years ago, such as Mobilization for Youth in New York's lower East Side, to new legal thresholds, such as the California Rural Legal Assistance Program which makes legal assistance a reality for many a migratory farm worker, to say nothing of Evanston's new office at 828 Davis—has been accompanied by emphasis on producing and monitoring change in the lives of those utilizing the services as well as in the norms that emerge from the regulatory agencies and the courts.

A prototype of the cases and doctrines emerging from the expansions of legal aid and the concomitant monitoring of them is the case of *In re Timoteo Raya*, decided in California's Third Appellate District Court of Appeals. In September, the Juvenile Court of Sacramento had ordered the removal of two children from the home of the natural mother because she had been living with a man other than her husband. Her informal union with a new partner had also resulted in three additional children. In the course of the husband's divorce proceedings against the children's mother, jurisdiction over the two children was given to the Juvenile Court, and the court in turn committed the children to the joint supervision of the Probation Office and the Welfare Department of Sacramento.

The Chief Counsel of the Legal Aid Society of Sacramento County filed an appeal challenging the authority of the Juvenile Court to remove the children from the natural mother's home. He argued in his brief that the mother and her new partner had established a stable home, that the children were properly cared for and doing well in school, and that the fact that the woman had never secured a divorce from her husband and hence was now in this legally "meretricious relationship" did not justify the removal of the children. The District Court of Appeals reversed the decision of the Juvenile Court, asserting in the course of its opinion that the Juvenile Court law was not intended to expose homes to "wholesale intervention by public authorities." The District Court of Appeals also found that poverty had played a major role in producing the home situation which had led the Juvenile Court to act.

Adequately financed couples can afford divorce. . . . The children of quicky marriages and quicky divorces need never find themselves in homes characterized by a permanent liaison such as Mrs. Raya's. For centuries the law has termed such liaisons meretricious or adulterous. Perhaps, in this day of casually created and broken marriages, the label should be applied with less readiness when poverty is a prime factor in producing the relationship. There is a danger here of imposing standards adapted to the well-to-do, who can usually pay for the forms of legitimacy, and ill-adapted for the poor, who frequently cannot . . . .[1]

Not the least significant aspect of the case is the fact that the appeal was commenced in September and its results published in the October issue of a bulletin with nation-wide circulation. There is maximum assurance that the decision will not lie buried in the advance sheets. The decision of the District Court of Appeals has had a significant effect, not only on Mrs. Raya and her family, for it is bound to become an important yardstick by which similar questions can be resolved in the future.

These California projects are by no means unique. The American Bar Foundation, under the grant from the Office of Economic Opportunity, has undertaken a study of legal services for the poor designed "to contribute to knowledge about the legal aid movement, the legal profession, the administration of justice, and problems of substantive and procedural law as they affect the poor, and to create an organized body of empirical data for future study and analysis by the American Bar Foundation, the Office of Economic Opportunity, and other appropriate agencies."[2] Field research has been completed in San Francisco, St. Louis, Miami, and Peoria, and a comprehensive and realistic profile of the availability of legal services of various types will soon be made public.

The scanning and integration of these projects and studies into systematic programs for continuing education are part of the function of the recently established National Institute for Education in Law and Poverty. Based at Northwestern University's School of Law and funded by the Office of Economic Opportunity, the purpose of the National Institute is "to develop a meaningful and relevant program of legal education to assist attorneys in providing quality representation for the poor." Conferences and publications of the Institute will review the basic laws affecting indigent clients and suggest those subjects and areas which appear ripe for challenge and innovation. Part of the curriculum will address itself to new techniques and legal theories, "both tried and untried." The National Institute will no doubt serve as a clearing house of information and ideas that can extend both the availability and quality of legal services for the poor.

The burgeoning of neighborhood legal centers and of studies and institutes to disseminate and evaluate the products of their work by no means guarantees adequacy of access for the poor to the judicial mechanism. But the fact that less than four million dollars was spent in 1963 to finance the civil case load of all legal aid organizations in the United States, whereas the Office of Economic Opportunity provided some forty million for legal services programs in fiscal 1967, provides a significant contrast between approaches to fulfilling the need for legal services. This carries no certainty, of course, that fulfillment has proceeded beyond tokenism. Eligibility tests, overburdening case loads, and hostile attitudes on the part of many local bar associations continue as impediments to success.

When pressure was brought on the Office of Economic Opportunity to relocate or dismiss the attorneys at California Rural Legal Assistance who challenged the Department of Labor's programs and processes, the answer of the Legal Services Program, supported by leaders of the American Bar Association, was simply to cite Canon 15 of the Canons of Professional Ethics:

The lawyer owes entire devotion to the interest of the client, warm zeal in the maintenance and defense of his rights and the exertion of his utmost learning and ability, to the end that nothing be taken or be withheld from him, save by the rules of law, legally applied. No fear of judicial disfavor or public unpopularity should restrain him from the full discharge of his duty.

I have discussed thus far the potentiality of access to the legal system. The major question in this tinder-box era, however, is the capacity of law to serve as an instrument of reform. Can law do something other than preserving the vested interests of power elites while occasionally soothing with verbal emollients the bruised psyches of random petitioners?

The answer is not yet definitive, though encouraging patterns are emerging. One major pattern consists of the re-examination and re-formulation of norms so as to enhance their congruence with reality. Another is the growing readiness, if not desire, on the part of the courts to test compliance with judicial norms through the examination of empirical data. This is not to say that the judiciary is creating legal norms that invariably reflect human behavior. There are some areas of the law such as negligence and pornography in which contemporary standards of reasonable behavior may frame the applicable judicial norm, but in areas such as segregation and other phases of equal protection and due process the "is's" of actual behavior do not create the "is's" of law. The norms proclaimed by the courts may well be designed to reform rather than reflect actual behavior.

Whether their norms were designed to conform to or to reform behavior, courts in the past were often content to ignore questions of whether their norms produced compliance or not. In more recent years the courts have been facing the compliance question realistically in order to enlarge law's capacity to change behavioral status quos. Let me illustrate by reference to shifts in the judiciary's perceptions about segregation in public education.

The evil wrought by the judiciary's formulation of the "separate but equal" concept in neutralizing the Fourteenth Amendment for three-quarters of a century was not embodied in the norm itself but in the refusal of the courts to examine empirical data that could show the violations of the norm.

Once having stated that segregated facilities were not unconstitutional so long as they were substantially equal, the courts then proceeded to ignore empirical standards for measuring equality. Even so stalwart a civil libertarian as John Marshall Harlan, who had dissented vehemently from the judicial acceptance of the "separate but equal" concept, was subsequently lulled into acquiescence in a case of overt denial of equal facilities to Negroes.

What is significant in our time is not the agonizing failure of the courts to act realistically following the adoption of the Fourteenth Amendment but rather that most of them are acting with regard to such reality today. The Brown case, of course, was the initial benchmark of the new wave. What is more significant than the Brown doctrine itself, though, is that it has sired profound judicial concern about compliance in practice with the norms proclaimed.

Such concern is not, of course, unanimous with all judiciaries. The Illinois Supreme Court decision last March in the Tometz case, declaring unconstitutional the state statute which had required school boards to " . . . change or revise existing units or create new units in a manner which will take into consideration the prevention of segregation and the elimination of separation of children in public schools because of color, race or nationality," provides a sobering jolt for those who thought that judicial preferences for the illusory have been abandoned. But while we must still reckon with such decisions, they are today's aberrations. Decisions such as Judge J. Skelly Wright's in *Hobson* v. *Hansen* requiring an end to de facto segregation in the District of Columbia carve the new benchmark.

The Hobson case is a benchmark not because the District of Columbia court is right and the Illinois court is wrong in its reading of law, but because the court in Hobson recognizes law's crucial role as an instrument of social change and asserts the judiciary's responsibility to make visible problems otherwise immune from public examination. Most significantly, Judge Wright sees the problem of segregation in the schools not merely as a matter of race but as a problem of the interrelationships of law and poverty.

In its examination of the evidence before enjoining the school board from operating the track system in the District of Columbia public schools and permanently enjoining discrimination on the basis of "racial or economic status" in the operation of public schools, the court examined in comprehensive detail plaintiff's argument that aptitude tests as currently constituted and interpreted discriminate against the disadvantaged child. The court accepts the finding that children with high socio-economic status as measured by the family's annual income, and high cultural status as measured by the number of years of schooling attained by parents, are likely to achieve higher test scores—not because of innate superiority but because the tests are geared to their level and mode of communication. In the case of the disadvantaged child, according to Judge Wright:

> Verbalization tends to occur less frequently and often less intensively. Because of crowded living conditions, the noise level in the home may be quite high with the result that the child's auditory perception—his ability to discriminate among word sounds—can be retarded. There tends to be less exposure to books or other serious reading material— either for lack of interest or lack of money.

The disadvantaged child has little or no opportunity to range beyond the boundaries of his immediate neighborhood. He is unfamiliar, therefore, with concepts that will expand both his range of experience and his vocabulary. He has less exposure to new things that he can reduce to verbal terms. For example, one defense witness, a principal of a low-income Negro elementary school, told of how most of the children had never been more than a few blocks from home; they had never been downtown, although some had been to a Sears department store, they did not know what an escalator was, had not seen a department-store Santa Claus, had not been to a zoo. These experiences, common in the subject matter of tests and textbooks, were alien to the lives of these children.[3]

The cultural biases of aptitude tests should not be allowed to decide who gets what kind of educational opportunity. A school system that presumes to tell a student what he can successfully learn incurs an obligation " . . . to be certain that it is in a position to decide whether the students' deficiencies are true, or only apparent."[4]

The District of Columbia court's meticulous probe of ecological factors that affect learning is a model, not necessarily of judicial accuracy nor of judicial self-righteousness, but rather of judicial methodology that insists upon relevance between constitutional norms and the empirical behavior of individuals, organizations and institutions. It recognizes that courts cannot be merely helpless observers or neutrals in the social conflicts of our age. That the courts in recent years have been both shield and sword for those who might otherwise suffer in silence is one positive indicator of law's capacity to involve the alienated and enhance commitments to the policy processes of democracy.

The recent enlargement of the right to privacy is an important manifestation of constitutional growth that has broad implications for the rights of the poor. The Griswold case declaring unconstitutional Connecticut's ban on contraceptives is not destined for fame because of the consequences of its substantive ruling; the substantive legal question had been behaviorally moot for many years since the law had not been enforced.[5] The more pregnant aspect of the case was the development of the principle of privacy. Justice Douglas contended in the court's decision that a constitutional right to privacy exists and that it is derived from the "penumbras" formed by emanations from the specific guarantees of the Bill of Rights. "Various guarantees create zones of privacy."[6]

Included are the right of association contained in the penumbra of the First Amendment; the prohibition against the quartering of soldiers in any house in time of peace without the consent of the owner, pursuant to the Third Amendment; and the "right of the people to be secure in their persons, houses, papers, and effects, against unreasonable searches and seizures" pursuant to the Fourth Amendment. Douglas also cited the Ninth Amendment as a source of the right to privacy although he did not state its explicit application.

Justice Goldberg's concurring opinion, placing more definitive reliance on the Ninth Amendment, insisted that the ordering and regulation of behavior by the state is permissible to the extent that fundamental personal rights are not infringed. Justice Harlan, in a concurring opinion, emphasized that the right protected was not merely that of home against intrusion but of "the life which characteristically has its place in the home." Asserting that it would be an extreme instance of sacrificing substance to form if the constitutional principle of privacy against official intrusion were held to comprehend only physical invasion by the police, Harlan concluded that the right to family privacy in the home is based only partially on the sanctity of property rights. More fundamental to the right of privacy is that "the home derives its pre-eminence as the seat of family life."[7]

Renewed emphasis was placed by Justice White this year on "the constitutional right to be free from unreasonable government invasions of privacy" in a decision ruling that the Fourth Amendment bars prosecution of a person who refuses to permit inspection of his personal residence for violation of the housing code when inspectors fail to obtain a warrant.[8] The Court also ruled that the requirement for an inspection warrant applies to commercial structures as well as to private residences. Justice White

23

stressed the importance of protecting privacy by preventing the decision to enter and inspect from being the product of the unreviewed discretion of the enforcement officer in the field.[9]

In a case argued before the Supreme Court in October 1967, the judges were urged to hold that the rule against unreasonable searches and seizures should not depend upon anachronistic property notions of trespass.[10] The Court was asked to adopt a new test based upon privacy rather than property rights. Counsel for the petitioner, seeking a ruling that the Fourth Amendment barred FBI agents from recording a gambler's conversations through a listening device placed on top of a public telephone booth, urged the Court to follow a "reasonable man" test. If a reasonable man would consider a conversation confidential in view of the setting, tone of voice, and activities involved, the Fourth Amendment should bar interceptions.

Such expansions of the right to privacy augur well for the dignity of the poor, who must deal with the parentalism and officiousness that reject privacy in the administration of housing, health, welfare, and law enforcement. If there is such a thing as a fringe to a penumbra, the changing legal position of the individual with "no visible means of support" would appear to be one. Emerging out of the penumbra-spawned right to privacy is the norm that vagrancy cannot be a crime. The succinct opinion of the New York Court of Appeals' ruling unconstitutional in July of 1967 the state's vagrancy statute stressed that "a statute whose effect is to curtail the liberty of individuals to live their lives as they would . . . must bear a reasonable relationship to . . . the alleged public good on account of which this restriction on individual liberty would be justified."[11] Finding that vagrancy statutes originated in feudal laws against runaway serfs and were designed as means of controlling the economic life of the populace, the court ruled that such coercive measures punishing status or a condition of being are inconsistent with widespread efforts in the present era to motivate and educate the poor toward economic betterment of themselves through the War on Poverty and its related programs.

Welfare and public health laws rather than criminal laws should be invoked, the court added, to cope with "alcoholic derelicts and other unfortunates, whose only crime, if any, is against themselves, and whose main offense usually consists in leaving the environs of Skid Row and disturbing *by their presence* the sensibilities of residents of nicer parts of the community."[12]

Judge Burke pointed out that the case raises an interesting equal-protection argument "as to whether persons of means are entitled any more than the poor to enjoy the allegedly debilitating effects of idleness." The formal basis on which the statute was invalidated, however, was that it violates due process by unreasonably making criminal the idleness of an individual that in no way impinges on the rights of others and has no more than the most tenuous connection with the preservation of public order. . . .

The theme stressed recurrently in this paper has been that of the potentiality of law to provide access to its mechanisms and processes for the indigent, and the potentiality, through such access, to change its norms and people's behavior. Numerous indicators attest to these potentialities: the more than 600 neighborhood legal offices established under Office of Economic Opportunity's Legal Services Program staffed by more than 1,200 full-time lawyers paid out of federal funds; judicial expansions of the constitutional right to counsel and development of the constitutional right to privacy; recognition on the part of the judiciary that compliance with judicial norms cannot be assumed but must be investigated systematically with the utilization of social science techniques; and the integration of professional skills, especially those of lawyers and social workers, in challenging substantive and procedural injustice. . . .

It seems clear, as Cloward and Piven pointed out recently, that nearly eight million Americans who depend on public assistance checks for their sustenance have become "the no-longer silent welfare poor."[13] But by any standards, the progress of the law in enhancing the dignity and self-respect of the poor and assaulting the arbitrary prejudice the poor traditionally face has been minute when contrasted with the magnitude of the task. It has been estimated, for example, that only one in four of our 32 million poor receive public welfare. A recent article by a California Rural Legal Assistance attorney on how to handle a welfare case refers accurately to welfare law practice as an "esoteric area" manned by a "meager legal army of the war on poverty who have ventured forth to battle the hitherto impregnable fortresses of the well-meaning enemies of the poor: bureaucracy, delay, silence and indifference."[14]

There is danger, too, that out of the quest for law reform and the inundation of Legal Services offices with clients' cases will emerge a system of selection of cases to be activated that could make the Legal Services Program just one more bureaucracy with which the poor have to cope. Perhaps the most heartless wrong that could be perpetrated on the poor would be to arouse expectations of redress and reform, only to have the expectations hopelessly mired in rituals and red tape. It is hard to see how these objectives can be achieved without some concomitant reorientation of our sense of values. I've often wondered, for example, how we could authorize special tax treatment for incomes produced by minerals, oil, and gas on the ground that these were "depletion allowances," whereas athletes, actors, or other humans whose resources diminish with age cannot qualify for the depletion allowance. A full-scale confrontation of poverty by law no doubt requires some challenges to the ideology of our tax structures as well as to more mundane matters of administering programs for the poor. The negative income tax which would pay out federal funds to those whose income falls below a minimum is certainly no more whimsical than one that rewards investors for the alleged depletion of resources that rarely in practice deplete. Equality before the law requires attention to a tax structure which calls upon low-income groups to bear an inordinate share of the tax burden.

Legislation enhancing the rights of debtors is another major item for the agenda. Debtor and creditor laws are still geared overwhelmingly to the advantage of the creditor. The opportunity for a creditor to have the remedy both of repossession and of a deficiency judgment on the repossessed items in a majority of states is but one example of how the law subordinates the interests of debtors.

The doctrine of unconscionability in contracts could and should become an important asset in the defense of debtors' rights, for high-pressure sales pitches and exorbitant prices are as prevalent today as ever. It is heartening that there have been a number of illustrations in the past several years of application of the concept of unconscionability as presently recognized in the Uniform Commercial Code. In situations in which excessive prices have been charged, courts have indicated that an otherwise valid contract can be invalidated as unconscionable. More significant than the isolated cases that have been decided on this theme is the potential of the Uniform Consumer Credit Code in process of preparation by the Commissioners on Uniform State Laws. Pursuant to the Consumer Credit Code, a contract would be declared unconscionable where there is a gross disparity between the price readily available in credit transactions in the geographic area and the price paid by the purchaser in the particular transaction.

There are, of course, other potential applications of unconscionability beyond excessive price. A seller's refusal to return repossessed goods after installment payments have been brought up to date by the buyer presents but one example. Unfortunately, the most sanguine optimist cannot contend that unconscionability provides a significant current remedy for the poor. Relief for the overburdened debtor must be obtained not so much through challenge to the contracts he signed as by resort to the bankruptcy court. Yet even the remedy of the bankruptcy proceeding can be illusory. The debtor in our bankruptcy courts is more often processed than served. Too often he emerges with a discharge, the contours and limits of which are unfamiliar to him. It really isn't anyone's fault—courts are crowded and lawyers are busy, and the newly discharged debtor frequently finds a sympathetic loan company or used car dealer waiting patiently for him to reaffirm an old debt or incur a new one, one which can't be avoided by another bankruptcy since a discharge can be obtained only once in six years. The bankruptcy courts are currently burdened by a case load in excess of 200,000 cases a year, and these do not include many of the nation's poor. If the poor were ever to join a mass campaign to resort to bankruptcy as an instrument of relief, it could wreck the system—an idea not wholly without merit.

This, then, is a report of progress and potentials,

providing a basis for further hopes and expectations rather than for satisfaction. It shows that there is ferment and change for the better, and that disputes that might otherwise have provoked violence in the streets are being brought into courtrooms and resolved there. Whether this is enough progress to forestall the rejection of constitutional processes as impotent and senile is within my range of hope but not of prediction. In a major sense, the law is competing with the revolutionaries in seeking the loyalty and participation of the alienated. Although this is not the kind of competition one ordinarily relishes, democracy can hardly thrive without it ❧

[1] *CEB Legal Services Gazette*, Vol. II, No. 1 (Oct. 1967), 12.

[2] Preliminary draft, American Bar Foundation Study of Legal Services.

[3] 269 *Federal Supplement* 401 (1967) at 481.

[4] *Ibid.*, p. 492.

[5] Griswold v. Connecticut, 381 U.S. 479 (1965).

[6] 381 U.S. 479 (1965), 484.

[7] *Ibid.*, at 551.

[8] Camara v. Municipal Court, 387 U.S. 523 (1967).

[9] 387 U.S. 541, at 545.

[10] Katz v. U.S., 36 *Law Week* (Oct. 24, 1967), 3165.

[11] Fenster v. Leary, 229 N.E. 2d 426 (1967) at 429.

[12] *Ibid.*, at 430.

[13] Richard A. Cloward and Frances Fox Piven, "We've Got Rights! The No-Longer Silent Welfare Poor," *New Republic*, 157 (Aug. 5, 1967), 23-27.

[14] Carol Ruth Silver, "How to Handle a Welfare Case," *Law in Transition Quarterly*, 4 (June 1967), 87-111.

The Difficult Road to Excellence

Percy L. Julian

Director of Julian Research Institute

In the sophistication of accumulated knowledge, we are richer than any generation the world has ever spawned. The scientific revolution of the past three decades has increased our knowledge of the physical world more than the preceding hundred years had done. Why, then, has this proliferation of human knowledge created confusion among scholars? Why should man's "divine discontent" with ignorance of his habitat create problems? Why should the farthest outreach of thought create any problems for humanity? Why should men wonder if the search for truth is the search for goodness? The answers, or partial answers, to these questions are at the very core of university education in these days of universal dissension, discord, and wholesale disagreement on ways out of the ugly blanket of fog that has descended upon the spirit of man. Let us see if we can examine a few of the possible answers in our search for the real "Road to Excellence."

First of all, most of us are greatly disturbed when too much newness descends upon us in too rapid a fashion. Most of us like the small simple worlds in which we live, our simple concepts, and the tidy order in which we have arranged our life and our day-to-day routine. Part of our confusion in this area arises from those who have bottled up their God and our universe in convenient compartments, in compact concepts that fit in neatly with their rationalizations. They cannot, in humility, conceive of the vastness in human outlook and the vastness in the concept of God, so necessary for humanity in this era. They cannot picture a world in harmony with man's noble dreams down the ages; they cannot even see realism or practicality in faithfully obeying even the ethical precepts to which they glibly give lip service. They cannot do all this because they cannot reconcile it with their own man-sized God—a God who fits into their convenient rationalizations, and who changes form and stature only with their change in outlook, if, indeed, their outlook ever changes, to say nothing of expanding. Thus, theirs is a devotion to half-truth; theirs is a devotion to one side of the truth; theirs is a devotion to the mere husks and rinds of the relevant and ennobling ideals that man has formed out of his sufferings through the ages. The real scholar must choose between a well-ordered static world and a world of buoyant change.

A second group which contributes to our confusion would bury all of the civilization and culture of the past. They would agree that the culture of the past is irrelevant. Humanity no longer sees its splendor mirrored in the tortuous struggles of the past. Indeed, for this group, the past is not prologue, for they have not cultivated a historical consciousness. This type of thinking and teaching can be one of the most dangerous of enemies in the educative process. If human history is to be considered as horses moving on a theatre stage but getting nowhere, then man is not maturing; rather, he is grasping at every straw which fits his restless whims, and ignoring all of the hard-earned safeguards which protect him against his most primitive instincts and leanings.

This group leans to the viewpoint that only that which is new is relevant, and for them there are no eternal verities. Thus, in this group, we find the ethical and moral relativists, the logical positivists, the radical pleasure seekers, and even the hard-core neo-racists. While they often claim to be non-conformists like Thoreau, their non-conformity often leaves a vacuum with nothing remaining that may give real hope and substance to the waning spirits of humanity. Their claim to "enlightened civilization" for many or most of their adherents is like that of a proverbial fading beauty who goes out and buys a new, incongruous, psychedelic dress, and has her face lifted to bolster something which does not exist. Or it resembles the mad search of a Ponce de Leon who thinks that by escaping from old reality he can find new youth. This group has no historical consciousness, and, indeed, if ever there were a need for greater development of this awareness in the educative process, that time is now.

30

Our forefathers thought that our system of liberal arts education would guarantee us a safeguard for future generations trained in the broad requirements for citizenship in a great democracy. The scholar would be the whole man who kept his eyes always on the stars, but who did not fall into the degrading wells at his feet; the whole man who, fired with humanistic mission, went out into the world of men and developed disciples, rather than withdrawing himself into a selfish arena to sit idly upon his stool of eminence and comfort, oblivious to the suffering around him.

But, as science gave us more things for comfort, more gadgets for pleasure, more media for non-intellectual and sensuous diversion, the lust for more things—mere things—became the dominant obsession of our age. Our dreams that our colleges would produce the whole man are in danger of being shattered. There is not the slightest shadow of a doubt that the overpowering motivation—and perhaps the creeping paralysis—in our education today is the development of marketable skills. Unless you who guide our youth can overcome this trend, it is doubtful that our educational system can develop in abundance those scholars who in Longfellow's almost forgotten words, "can hear and feel the throbbing heart of man." The pitiful result is the oft-heard axiom that morality is as difficult to define as is the color yellow. If this is true, upon what basis shall our legislatures and our courts propound and interpret the laws to guide human behavior?

Far too many philosophers tell us that as long as man believed in a universe governed by a fatherly God, the world was a friendly habitat for him; for no matter how great the evil in the world, the good would always triumph. But science, they say, has taught us that the world about us is completely blind to good and evil; that the world is completely indifferent to our values. They further tell us that science has taught us that the universe is purposeless; that man's ideals and morals are but inventions of the mind, and that the universe outside man does not support or offer any basis for these ideals at all. Man is, therefore, alone and friendless in an indifferent world. God and religion are dead—killed by the revelations of science.

As a scientist, I cannot buy all of this, but it will take another visit to give my answer in entirety. Briefly put, we are admitting, with this frustration, that our concept of God and a purposefulness to man's endeavors were merely similar to the Santa Claus stories we tell our children. Beyond the fact that we still get along well with old Santa, this denigration of the concept of God by the mere expansion of human knowledge denigrates man to an extent that to me is unpalatable. It not only destroys the majesty of the human will, but makes of man nothing but an immature imbecile.

What, then, are the scholar's choices? We must superimpose the majesty of the human will upon the utilization of all truth, that truth may never be feared by mankind. As a corollary, there must be new definitions of morality, new primarily in that their concern is a preservation (and enhancement) of the humanistic gains of the ages. A simple example in this direction is the concept of rule by majority. This concept has degenerated into the false idea that the majority owns the rights of the minority, to be parceled out to the minority according to the whims of the majority. Indeed, the majority is not even the custodian of those rights; it is only the responsible purveyor, pledged to dispense them with honor or to be criminals in the face of the Law. Finally, we must enrich our concept of God to the end that man regain that type of humility which befits his station and his mortality in the vastness of our universe.

The decisive answer to all these semantic inquiries about the term "God" and the concept of God was really given by a wise old man of two thousand and more years ago. In Book III of Plato's *Republic* is recorded a conversation which we seem to have forgotten. Glaucon, the pupil, says to his teacher: "Socrates, as to this City of God which you command me to establish, and whose tenets you command me to obey—I do not believe that such a City of God exists anywhere on earth." And Socrates answers him by saying: "Glaucon, whether such a City of God exists in Heaven, or ever will exist on earth, the wise man will pattern himself after the manner of that city, having nothing to do with any other, and in so looking upon it, will set his own house in order " ❧

Greetings

. . . from the State of Illinois

Samuel H. Shapiro

Governor of Illinois

Education is the single most important product of government. It is also the single most important necessity for a free and democratic state and nation. Education is the reason that I stand where I stand today, just as it is the reason that so many of the rest of these distinguished leaders are here with me. More importantly, education is the reason that the United States ranks in the world community where it does today.

Northern Illinois University has a rich history under the leadership of five successive educators of learning and experience. The challenges of our increasingly sophisticated and complex society are such that each in turn has been called upon to face greater challenges and carry heavier burdens than his predecessor. It is a measure of these men that each has been equal to the task ❧

34

...from the Federal Government

Willard Wirtz

United States Secretary of Labor

It is my assignment—and privilege—to bring greetings from the Federal Government upon the inauguration of President Rhoten Smith. But since government is simply the means through which people do for and with each other those things which require some organizational effort, my greetings are from no separate entity, but from two-hundred million Americans. Thinking about those two-hundred million people and about your inaugural theme, "Excellence and Opportunity," or "quality education for the many," I wonder what would happen if we woke up tomorrow to find our dream of an excellent education for everyone come true. I have no doubt that the nation's affairs would grind to a halt within a week. This is because education creates expectations and entitlements far beyond the capacity of our present society to satisfy. The solution to this paradox is not, of course, to slow down on education or to aim short of our goal of universal, quality education. I think of Don Quixote, singing in *Man of La Mancha:* it is our duty—nay our privilege—to dream the impossible dream, to pursue the impossible star. Instead, the answer is to develop in our society a social structure—an economic and political system—which provides not only the universal opportunity for an excellent education, but also the opportunity to satisfy the desires and expectations that an excellent education creates ❧

...from the Faculty of Northern Illinois University

Paul S. Burtness

Professor of English

It is an honor to have been selected by the University Council to bring the greetings and best wishes of the faculty to you, Dr. Smith, on this signal occasion of your inauguration as sixth president of Northern Illinois University.

I am not going to speak about the phenomenal quantitative expansion that has occurred at this institution in recent years. I do not intend to emphasize the fact that in Illinois the Regency Universities System ranks second in size only to the University of Illinois System, nor the fact that this campus at DeKalb ranks second in size only to that at Urbana. Such physical and numerical growth is impressive, to be sure. Indeed, to those of us who have been privileged to participate, it seems almost incredible.

Among the faculty at this university now, however, there are enthusiasm and optimism grounded on far more important considerations and looking toward vastly more significant goals than merely continued expansion of facilities and increased numbers of staff and students.

39

May I take a moment to draw your attention to a few of the considerations that lead many of us to look to the future with such confidence and high hope.

First, as a consequence of President Smith's leadership during the present academic year, there is emerging a sense of the essential coherence which is proper for a university, a sense of a unifying commitment to learning and rational inquiry. Students, faculty members, and officers of administration are gradually developing the feeling of being engaged in a joint effort—a common effort—with the result that communication and understanding among these diverse constituencies are demonstrably improving. The concept of appropriately shared responsibility—not more than a dream or a slogan at many schools—is beginning to provide a flexible technique for enhancing the quality of decisions and cooperation throughout the university.

Second, with President Smith's bold encouragement, the faculty are viewing their responsibilities as teachers and scholars with kindled imagination and a renewed appreciation of the essential interaction that must occur between teaching and searching if the process of instruction is to be truly vital. All of us are being encouraged to innovate, to experiment, to challenge the student to achieve to the limit of his capabilities. And this spirit is contagious. I discern a growing dedication to excellence in the studies and activities of increasing numbers of our students.

Third, a renaissance in intellectual and cultural vitality is manifest throughout the university community. It is manifest in the deliberations of the University Council, in our new Honors program, in our improving library collections. It is manifest in the number and quality of musical and dramatic performances, lectures, and exhibitions occurring on campus. It is manifest too in the creative activity of faculty and students alike, and in the creation of our ambitious university press. Our acquisition of the Alexander Calder stabile *Le Baron* represents, in a profound sense, this new commitment by the university community to beauty, creativity, innovation, and excellence.

Fourth, regarding the larger context of higher learning in Illinois, we at Northern Illinois University have been greatly heartened by the vision and expertise of the Board of Higher Education in developing its outstanding Master Plan, which coordinates systems of colleges and universities into one comprehensive system. As a result, excellence in higher education will be recognized and encouraged more equitably throughout the state. The wisdom of the Illinois legislature in supporting the Master Plan has been exemplary. In recruiting faculty talent and in retaining it in Illinois, the importance of such long-range planning by the Board and of such enlightened support by the legislature cannot be overstated.

Fifth, the establishment of our present governing body—the Board of Regents—and the appointment to it of distinguished leaders from science, medicine, technology, education, and civic life are sources of pride to all of us here at DeKalb. The skill and devotion of the Regents —their willingness to work in close cooperation with the universities, both with the presidents and with elected representatives of the faculties—impress me as being virtually unique in the governance of American universities. The Regents are a source of inspiration for all of us to do our very best.

Finally—and most important of all—is the fact that Rhoten Smith accepted our invitation last May to join us at Northern Illinois and to provide leadership in our quest for higher opportunities of service, for fuller realization of our potentialities, and for greater achievement of excellence ❧

The Sixth President

Investiture

Norris L Brookens

Chairman of the Board of Regents

Rhoten A. Smith, the excellence of your attainments has brought you to the presidency of Northern Illinois University, and thus to the opportunity of guiding this institution in the adventurous years ahead. This university stands on the proposition that the life of reason and civility provides the best hope for meeting the issues which confront our society today. Indeed, our recognition of the scholarly distinction and high purpose of your career is largely responsible for our calling you to your new position of leadership.

We charge you today to dedicate your imagination, your intellect, and your energy to the realization of the highest potentialities of which this university is capable, and to the fulfillment of its new mission. We charge you to provide the leadership which will enable Northern Illinois University to discover new challenges, new avenues of service. Though none of us can know the future, we are confident that under your presidency this university will reach new levels of excellence.

Accordingly, by the authority vested in me as chairman of the Board of Regents, I hereby invest you with the authority of the presidency of Northern Illinois University. Let this medallion, used for the first time today, symbolize your continuing responsibilities. May all your endeavors bear witness to those imperatives, sanctioned by tradition, that this ceremony represents. Serve well, serve long, and seek always to serve excellence and opportunity. ❧

46

Inaugural Address

Excellence and Opportunity

Rhoten A. Smith

The theme of today's inauguration occurred to me last fall when I heard President Fred Harrington of the University of Wisconsin speak. He talked about the way in which the pendulum swings in public higher education between the desire for excellence and the desire for providing opportunity. In choosing this as my theme, I have deliberately chosen a dilemma: Excellence *and* Opportunity.

The two concepts do pose something of a dilemma, because the achievement of genuine educational excellence, difficult though it may be, is undeniably possible if one had enough money and were in a position to ignore the urgent need in today's society for the expansion of educational opportunity. Similarly, a university such as ours can contribute very significantly to expanded educational opportunity—indeed it has dramatically done so over the last decade—but that contribution becomes far more difficult when it must be accompanied by qualitative improvement in the educational experience of all our students. So the twin goals of excellence and opportunity do

49

pose a dilemma, but a dilemma that this institution and our whole system of higher education in this country are going to have to face.

The theme of "excellence" is one which has been widely used by educators in the last few years. There is little doubt about what we usually mean by academic excellence, or even about how it can be achieved. If an institution attracts students with high academic potential and background, and the best faculty talent, and places them in desirable facilities with modern equipment and a first-class library, the result is going to be high-quality education and the institution will be one of recognized excellence.

After the shock of Sputnik in 1957, the nation responded strongly, making great effort to improve American education from kindergarten through the doctoral level. The conjunction of this national effort and steeply rising enrollments made it possible for a number of our public institutions, particularly the large state universities, to become more selective in admitting students, to attract outstanding faculty members, and to provide the conditions necessary for academic excellence. At the same time, the former state teachers' colleges, like this institution, were also given greatly increased support, enabling us not only to grow dramatically, but to develop into universities with a multiple educational mission.

Just how astonishingly this university has grown in

the last two decades can be illustrated by looking back to our last inauguration in 1949, when Leslie A. Holmes was installed as the fifth president of NIU. At that time we had approximately 1,600 students. Eight years later that number had tripled, and in the next ten years we quadrupled in size again—a twelvefold growth in eighteen years. In later years Dr. Holmes remembered with a smile that he had been amazed at his own audacity in predicting in his inaugural address an enrollment of 2,500 by 1960. He had hedged this prediction by saying that this growth would be possible only if adequate resources and facilities were provided by the state.

Thus, the determination of the people of Illinois to meet the state's educational responsibilities has enabled Northern Illinois University to grow in size and to develop in quality and diversity to a degree which could not be predicted twenty years ago. But though there has been measurable improvement in quality over the past decade, it is clear that we have made our greatest contribution in the area of opportunity—in the way in which we have expanded rapidly to meet as nearly as possible the demands of students for education beyond the high school.

In the years immediately ahead we shall continue to make this contribution to educational opportunity. NIU will doubtless continue to grow, although probably not at the same headlong pace, and our efforts will be expanded more and more at the junior-senior and graduate levels and less, proportionately, at the freshman-sophomore level. But opportunity in today's troubled world means more than just continuing growth in numbers of students.

Up until fifty years ago, the higher educational system of this country could be content with serving the economic and social elite. Others did not generally aspire to higher education. For the last fifty years, and until very recently, the national system of higher education has put its emphasis on serving the intellectual elite. Our universities became, in the words of Christopher Jencks and David Riesman, "meritocratic institutions"—institutions to serve the high academic achievers among our young people.

A college education has now come to seem, however, almost indispensable for success in life; it appears to be the passport to future achievement, and though all who possess it will not achieve success, fewer and fewer will succeed without it in the years ahead. Knowledge of this prospect has helped to create the insistent demand that higher education expand in order to accommodate those growing numbers of diploma-hungry (and hopefully learning-hungry) students.

A college diploma can really be the passport to achievement, to influence and affluence, to leadership in twentieth-century America. Thus it has acquired an immense importance and attraction, doubly so for those who have largely been excluded by our society from achievement and influence and affluence and leadership. And if it be true that ghetto education and the texture of life in the slums prepare one rather for failure than for success, the question arises as to the responsibility of society to act to eradicate these inequities. It is my conviction that the universities can and must change their thinking about how one comes to higher education. The public universities, especially, can and must find ways to make more widely available opportunities for earning this passport to the good life. To fail to do so is to bar the door to a hopeful future in the very faces of those of our citizens who have least to hope for from life. Our abundant society cannot afford to bar that door.

The proposal to expand opportunity in the way I have been suggesting brings the dilemma between excellence and opportunity into sharp focus. Harold Howe II, United States Commissioner of Education, recently illuminated this dilemma succinctly when he said: "Entirely too many colleges have, in the name of maintaining standards, fenced out the children of the poor and the victims of discrimination."

To be perfectly clear about expanding educational opportunity to those who have the greatest need for it, let me say that I am *not* suggesting a lowering of standards. To lower entrance standards would likely lead to another failure for these students. I *am* suggesting, first, that students who have the ability be sought out and recruited by methods more sensitive than the usual tests of probable success in college. And second, it seems clear we will need to establish special counselling and study-help programs to deal with the special problems these students inevitably encounter in the university.

What is needed is not a double standard of grading or retention—one for black and one for white; one for the poor and another for the comfortably-fixed. What *is* proposed is, for example, a plan of six-year programs for the baccalaureate degree instead of the traditional four-year programs, which might assist in overcoming the deficiencies of earlier preparation and would help produce a graduate just as qualified as any other to fulfill a productive role in society.

What we must do, in sum, is to look more imaginatively at our admission procedures, our counselling and advising programs, our financial assistance program, and at our curriculum to see if there are not ways in which we can awaken latent abilities in *all* our students, regardless of their backgrounds or their educational objectives. If the problem is so viewed and so approached, I believe we can expand educational opportunity at this institution in a really exciting way without raising the specter of "lowered standards."

Now, just as the concept of opportunity can be broadened, so can our approach to excellence be creatively revitalized. Thus far, excellence has been achieved by our better public institutions under the formula mentioned earlier: good faculty plus good students plus good facilities. Basically that is the way it has been done, and we must continue to work on all three factors of the equation at NIU.

This university has succeeded well in attracting good faculty. In the matter of retaining the very best people there is room for improvement. This has been one of my primary goals this year. Time will test our ultimate success in improving our record of faculty retention, but I have been impressed with the recruiting skill of our departments and am confident that the good quality of our faculty will continue to improve.

In referring to good facilities as a necessary element in the achievement of excellence, I am speaking of buildings—offices and laboratories—of libraries, and of all the other physical equipment needed to sustain and support a complex educational enterprise. The State of Illinois, through its Board of Higher Education and through its governors and legislatures, has made a major effort to meet its obligations to provide higher education for its citizens by providing adequate facilities. One cannot walk about this campus and observe what has happened, especially in the last five years, without being aware of this effort. It has been difficult, and currently it is becoming even more difficult, to keep pace with what is needed. Still, one cannot seriously doubt that the facilities necessary for achieving excellence will continue to be provided.

But what of the students? Over the past few years the quality of our student body has clearly improved. Our admission policy, however, has been essentially one-dimensional (relying almost solely on the upper-half-of-the-graduation-class criterion) and highly mechanical in its application. We have, to some extent, tied our own hands. It can be demonstrated, I believe, that we turn away some students who are better than some we admit because our own rules have prevented us from using sensitive judgment.

All this is being changed by a new university committee on admissions. We will soon have a policy that is far more flexible, that will enable us to exercise judgment and capitalize on experience as well as on supposedly objective criteria, and that will produce a student body of increasingly impressive ability.

At the same time, we must have special portals for at least two kinds of students who often are screened out by mechanical selection methods. One of these is the disadvantaged youth of high ability, about whom I have already commented. Another is the returning veteran. All our experience with the returning veterans of World War II and the Korean War indicates that the usual criteria to measure success in college do not apply to this group. High motivation, maturity, and willingness to work are characteristics often found in the returning veteran, and these characteristics, we know, can outweigh those factors measurable by test scores or high school grades. With one hundred thou-

sand citizens of this state in the armed services, and with perhaps 80 per cent of them expected to continue their education when they return, we may soon see an influx of returning veterans which will not only tax our facilities but may usher in another exciting era in higher education like that which followed World War II.

But doing our best to get good students, good faculty, and good facilities will not in itself produce the excellence we at NIU all desire. A time of reckoning for higher education is upon us, and the danger for young universities such as ours is great. By the same token, we have an unparalleled opportunity.

The greatest problem is that the money needed to achieve the quality institution we want will probably not be sufficient if we approach excellence only in the traditional way. The nation has been generous with higher education for the last decade, and to a large extent it has been *uncritically* generous. This unquestioning open-handedness cannot continue. The institution which addresses itself to the question of productivity, and seeks valid ways of increasing productivity while enhancing quality, must fare better in the future than the institutions which have to be starved into examining their traditional ways of doing things. As a growing and as yet unfossilized institution, Northern Illinois University has an opportunity which older and more firmly established institutions do not have. I have elsewhere said that, sooner or later, higher educa-

tion, like any other segment of the economy, must increase its productivity to a degree commensurate with its advancing costs. Whether this is accomplished through imaginative use of technological aids or in some other manner, it will have to be accomplished. I shall not dwell further on this, but it is an item which will be high on our agenda in the years ahead.

Another of the complex problems faced by higher education is in the area of graduate education—the very area in which this institution will make its major contribution in the future. Criticisms of traditional graduate education, particularly at the doctoral level, have been loud and insistent for several years now. Complaints of undergraduates about the relevance of their courses and the quality of teaching in the universities have become more and more common, and the root of these complaints can be traced in large part to the nature of graduate training. Despite these criticisms, the traditional graduate schools appear literally to lack the capacity to change. Our graduate programs, because they are in their infancy, can be different, can be better, can set new directions, if only we have the courage, indeed, the audacity (for it will require an audacious spirit), to be different.

Without creating a false distinction between teaching and research, we can make preparation for teaching at the college and university level an integral part of graduate education. Furthermore, we must revolutionize the instructional process, finding new and far more effective ways to impart knowledge and stimulate thinking. For the student of the future will be measured less by his store of knowledge than by his ability to think and communicate. Factual information he acquires will have to be discarded more than once in his lifetime. Learning, then, will be a lifetime process, and formal schooling must become training for a life of learning and relearning.

Northern Illinois University undertakes its new mission just at the time when new and revolutionary changes in higher education are certain to come. These changes will come because their hour has come, and for too long we have ignored the need for change. Thus we find ourselves in a position where we can assume leadership in forging what I shall call the New University.

—The New University I foresee will make better use of its resources, especially human talent, the ingredient which gives an institution its character. Better understanding of the human learning process and technological innovations will lead to great changes in the instructional program, but the gain in productivity will free professors for more intensive and more meaningful contacts with students.

—The New University will see the coming of age of the social sciences and will consequently find itself much more involved in the solution of social problems.

—The undergraduate curriculum in the New University will feature more and more multidisciplinary work, less training for specific vocations, more attention to education for life in a world where change will be the only constant. In the New University the great bulk of the students will be transfers from junior colleges, and as many as half of the students will be going on for post-baccalaureate professional or graduate work.

—The New University will be dedicated equally to research and teaching—to the discovery of knowledge and the guiding of the young into lives of study, regardless of their vocational objectives. And it will cease to argue about the relative importance of the two, for it will be recognized that they are complementary functions.

—The New University will be a true collegium, with decisions resulting more from close cooperation and communication among faculty, students, administration, and the board than from confrontations based on conflict.

—With closer communication, and with more openness and more candor on the part of all, the New University will have less hostility and suspicion among its various segments than seems to be the case too often today. At the same time, the New University will be a place of intellectual ferment and controversy, with respect for the opinions of all *restored* as the basis of intellectual exchange.

—If all of this comes about, I believe the New University will once again claim the prideful allegiance of its faculty, students, and alumni, as colleges and universities once did. But this pride will be based not on nostalgia, sentiment, and football victories, but on continuing participation in the life of the mind.

In this year of the Sesquicentennial Anniversary of the State of Illinois, it is appropriate that we look toward the future, for that is the spirit of Illinois. And Northern Illinois University, as the state university located in the fastest developing and most promising region of Illinois, finds that spirit of high confidence in the future entirely congenial. Here, on these plains, will develop a New University, a university dedicated to both excellence and opportunity. To the task of building that New University I enthusiastically join with my colleagues now in laying our hands ❧

Commitments to Excellence

The Inauguration Motif

The inauguration motif embodies in circular form the initials of the university. Designed by Professor William T. Brown of the Department of Art especially for use during the inauguration activities, it will continue to inspire Northern Illinois University's renewed commitment to scholarship and service. Suggestive of the paradox underlying all art, its kinetic components (the figure must be revolved in order to reveal the initials) bespeak the dynamic nature of an energetic modern university, while its static simplicity betokens oneness, the achieved stillness of all artistic creations, including the *universitas* itself, whose Latin name is derived from *universus*, meaning "the whole." Its circular form, traditionally an emblem of perfection and consummation, suggests that academic traditions and contemporary social concerns are both best fulfilled in contexts of superior quality and imagination ❧

The Presidential Medallion

The presidential medallion displays the initials of the university and a nineteen-karat star ruby corresponding to its traditional color. The six-ounce, five-and-a-half-inch contemporary art object was created in wax and cast in fourteen-karat yellow gold by the centrifugal casting process. It will be worn by President Smith for the first time at the inauguration ceremony, and thereafter at commencements and other academic functions, and will be transferred to his successors in office. The medallion was commissioned by the Presidential Inauguration Committee and was executed by Professor Eleanor Caldwell of the Department of Art ❧

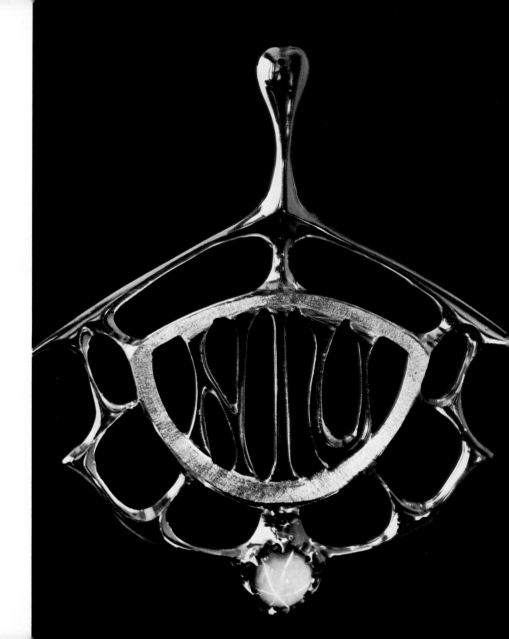

"Le Baron"

The acquisition of "Le Baron," Alexander Calder's impressive stabile of nickel steel plate, not only commemorates the inauguration of Rhoten A. Smith, but also marks a milestone in the cultural development of the university he has been called to lead. Symbolizing the new era that Northern Illinois University has entered and the imaginative thrust of its new mission, this major monument to excellence in all forms provides an important opportunity for the people of this community to see it tangibly manifest in their midst.

The seventy-year-old American sculptor for many years has commanded a distinguished international reputation as an innovative developer of the mobile and stabile, distinctively contemporary art forms. Located in the mall area of the campus, "Le Baron" stands sixteen feet high and fourteen feet wide. Its purchase was made possible by gifts to the Northern Illinois University Foundation, whose "Commitment to Excellence" development program is intended to attract to the campus additional works of art and other contributions in the adventurous years ahead. ❧

This book was edited by Arra M. Garab of the Department of English, Northern Illinois University, and was designed by William T. Brown of the Department of Art. The photographs were taken by Douglas Stewart of the Department of Art and David Repp of University Relations. The text was set in twelve-point Bodoni Book with display type in Garamond Bold italic. The paper is 80 lb. Warren Cameo Brilliant Dull Enamel. The book was printed by University Graphics, Aurora, Illinois, and bound by Brock and Rankin, Chicago.